Praise for *How Not to Pull Your Life Apart Caregiving*

Carroll is a well-respected thought leader in our industry. Her experience working for insurance companies, in distribution (sales) and now in public policy and consumer advocacy gives her a holistic view and insights into LTC Planning. I'm a friend and fan of her work -- I appreciate the advice and tactical steps to have more meaningful conversations with family members and clients.

- Steve Cain, National Sales & Business Development Leader, LTCI Partners

If you count yourself among the millions of families worried you are unprepared for the financial and emotional challenges of caregiving, you couldn't find a better guide than Carroll Golden. Informed by her remarkable career and firsthand experiences, Carroll uses personal stories to illustrate her practical, 3-step guide to caregiving and financial stability. Readers will know they are in the company of not just an expert, but someone who cares passionately about long-term care.

- Stephen D. Forman, CLTC, Senior Vice President, Long Term Care Associates, Inc.

This book has been such a lifeline for me and my family. The author's roadmap is an incredibly well-thought-out and caregiver-centric plan. This book fully acknowledges how intricate family relationships can complicate the process of coming up with a loved one's care plan. For me, the most challenging aspect of being a caregiver was finding myself thrust into that role with little forethought about what it would truly entail. The author's road map walks you through the process of having that first conversation about what information is needed to provide your loved one with the right care at the right time, as well as assigning roles and responsibilities within the family and planning for the start of care. I identified with several of the family stories in her book which really helped me to see how common of a struggle this is.

The author's guidance helps in addressing a common concern among caregivers who want to give their loved one the best possible care, without losing themselves and other family relationships in the process. I'll definitely be reading this book again as well as recommending it to others who are going through similar situations.
- Ivana Sheppard, GenX Mom and Caregiver

Once, again, Carroll's words are GOLDEN, continuing the conversation that is becoming more and more relevant... and necessary. An indispensable resource for millions of families as they face, and care for, society's aging population. Share it with your family, friends, clients and colleagues.
- Bryon Holz, CLU, ChFC, LUTCF, CASL, LACP
40-year Financial Advisor

Ms. Golden's book is a tangible guide for all of us to be prepared for the aging "gift of life." I'm really pleased that my husband Gordon and I have a jump start by having LTC insurance, an Estate Plan with a will, a living will, and a designated executor. It did, however open my eyes to other personal information that will also be needed when one of us passes before the other, or both at the same time. Your "Care Guide" with the "Content List" is loaded with valuable apps and suggestions.

This book also gives easy to follow steps to explore in the "The Care Guide," and " Care Planning Team." The numerous reflective stories, throughout the book, are people who shared how they used, or desperately needed to have the conversation and then plan to effectively care and assist their family/ friends in need. Your book has also encouraged me to have a conversation with my neighbor, Mary. If something should happen to her, I have no emergency information to help her or her family. We spend a lot of time together, and I need to know what she wants me to do in an emergency.

- Suzan Rothamel, Retired Teacher

Whether you are experiencing a caregiving need for a loved one or know you will someday, Carroll's book is a must read. I have worked with Carroll long before the books and the knowledge that she brings to her area of expertise from personal caregiving to planning for herself and her family to growing distribution in the long-term care industry and lending her knowledge to many associations surrounding insurance and caregiving, she knows what she's talking about. I know I enjoyed reading the book and I hope many others do as well as it will make the caregiving journey a bit more tolerable.

- Angie Hughes, LTCP, Managing Partner, Producers XL

I've been captivated by Ms. Golden's work in long-term care planning, especially her innovative approach to caregiving conversations. I found her discussion on the multifaceted aspects of caring for aging loved ones in the LifeBlood podcast episode "Planning for Caregiving with Carroll Golden" particularly insightful. Her insights and dedication to understanding both the financial and emotional complexities of caregiving resonate with themes focused on Family Wellness, Financial Planning, and Health Advocacy. Given the breadth and depth of her insights, her contributions, and her books significantly enrich diverse discussions.

- Josef Schinwald, MIB, MDiv Guest Experts on Air

Taking the guesswork out of "How Not To Pull Your Life Apart Caregiving" is Carroll's gift to the world in this practical yet dynamic book. "You only have two choices when it comes to caregiving: plan or panic." Thankfully, Carroll's roadmap for her reader helps one to plan and not panic. It is the GPS of all things practical about caregiving. From personal real-life stories to helpful and implementable steps, the reader is entrusted to manage the care of their loved ones because this book is a step-by-step guide for the caregiver to reach the desired outcome for them and their loved ones. It honors the legacy of the one being cared for and the one doing the caring!

> - Dr. Towera Loper, Leadership, Career, Life Coach. T.L. Loper and Consulting, LLC.

Having dealt with caregiving professionally and personally, I have firsthand knowledge of the complexities surrounding this topic. The unflinching and honest look offered got to the heart of the matter and allowed me to grow in acceptance and understanding. I encourage readers to approach this book as a fundamental tool in the journey from good intentions to a solid real-world plan.

> - Dan Mangus, Vice President Growth and Development, Senior Marketing Specialists, an Integrity Partner

Proactively planning for extended or long-term care is difficult, but not as difficult as making emergency care decisions under stress or when family members disagree. In addition, not all siblings can or equally pull their weight. If you're the primary caregiver for a parent, this book provides examples and tools for the conversations needed to gain a sense of control and protect your health, wealth, and family relationships.

> - Betty Meredith, CFA®, CFP®, CRC®, President, Retirement Speakers Bureau

Carroll Golden has written a book for every caregiver, which Rosalyn Carter correctly stated will be everyone at some time in their life. I, too, have written such books and so what makes Carroll's book a must read? Carroll, with her extensive knowledge of financial issues takes the reader through a clear and concise evaluation of many, if not all, the possible financial products that one should consider or use in their long-term care planning. This is a gold mine. If you are fortunate to be reading this book before the crisis situation, you will be so glad you did. But wait…there's more…. Carroll through her personal experience gives you concrete solutions to the ever-troubling family dynamic that surrounds caregiving. You NEED this book.

- Cathy Sikorski, Esq. National Speaker, Author, *12 Conversations: How to Talk to Almost Anyone About Long-Term Care Planning.*

Carroll is able to bring to the forefront the caregiver challenges so many women face today. The stories are immensely helpful and eye opening in bringing an understanding of the immediate need for all of us to start talking with family members about how to manage caregiving as we age. While a difficult conversation, it is the most important one that emotional and financially effects every member of a family. This book will help you start those necessary conversations.

- Christine McCullugh, President, LTC Solutions, Inc

How Not to Pull Your Life Apart Caregiving

Overcome Challenges and Objections to Planning Conversations

by Carroll S. Golden

Published 2024 by Corner Office Books
Printed in the United States of America

EAN-13: 979-8-9894863-2-8

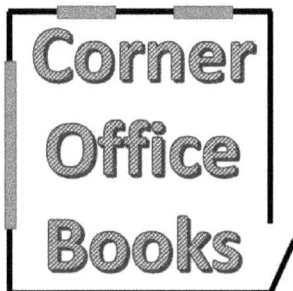

Corner
Office
Books

Dedication

My family is both caring and supportive. I have two exceptional children, Erik and Nicole, who appreciate my desire to help other families prepare for a financially stable, loving future. They help me see the caregiving and financial challenges their generation is facing, which I might otherwise not appreciate.

I have a kind, thoughtful daughter-in-law, Jodi, who devotes herself to raising my grandchildren, Carolyn and James, so they will understand that helping others and being a good family, community, and team member is a fulfilling way to live life. She learned it from her wonderful parents, John and Carol.

I am lucky to have two caring sisters, Patty and Debbi, and their husbands, Vic and Doug. I am grateful for the lessons we learn about generational and long distant caregiving challenges.

In loving memory, we dedicate this book to our mother. Our mother created an extended care plan so that many years later, when she became chronically ill, we enjoyed and supported her instead of fighting about caregiving challenges with each other.

Acknowledgements

Caregiving can be a rewarding but lonely and confusing place. I want to thank all those who generously shared their personal or family stories about the challenges they faced in discussing or implementing an extended care plan.

The extended and long-term care industry is a relatively small community of people made up of very dedicated, caring, and intelligent individuals. I am grateful for the many years of education, loyal friendships, and innovative contributions continually afforded me by that community and by my participation in the Intercompany Long Term Care Insurance Conference (ILTCI).

Advocating for extended and long-term care can be a challenging task. However, the team at the National Association of Insurance and Financial Advisors (NAIFA) has a Center of Excellence devoted to it which allows us to keep up-to-date on important legislation, proposals, studies, task forces, and initiatives that impact individual and family extended care planning.

Many friends and colleagues helped and encouraged me in writing this book. Special thanks to: Nicole Stuart, Steve Cain, Suzanne Carawan, Dan Mangus, Joe Dowdall, Angie Hughes, Christi Trimble, Steve Forman, Bryon Holz, Tom Michel, Towera Loper, Annalee Krueger, Betty Meredith, Diane Boyle and Martha Underwood for their contribution, collaboration, feedback, and encouragement.

I am indebted to my published, Donna Cavanagh, for her guidance, sense of humor, and wise suggestions which made this book immeasurably better.

Disclaimer

Neither the author nor the other contributors offer this information as tax, legal, investment, retirement advice, or recommendations. The content is derived from sources believed to be accurate. Neither the information presented nor any opinion expressed constitute a solicitation for the purchase or sale of any product or security. Interpretation of planning tools, suggestions, or products is used in the context of stories or experience, but may be suitable for other planning situations as well. All interpretations are subject to individual financial, legal, tax advice or family situations.

Please consult a professional advisor, investment advisor, tax consultant, or attorney before making a tax-related investment, insurance, or planning decision.

Table of Contents

Dedication I

Acknowledgements II

Disclaimer III

Introduction 1

    How to Use This Book 3

Shadow Caregiving System: The What, Who, When, Why, and How 4

Section I 9

Chapter 1: What's in a Name 10

Chapter 2: A Three Step Roadmap 12

    Step One: Care Guide: The "I Care and Respect You" Conversation 12

    Step Two: Care Squad: The "What If" Conversation 13

    Step Three: Care Planning Team: The "Discovery" Conversation 14

Chapter 3: A Bumpy Journey 16

    A Friend's Story 16

    Smoothing out the bumps, one step at a time 17

    Lyndsay's Story 17

Chapter 4: Caregivers Are Us 19

    Are you a participant in the Shadow Caregiver System? 19

    Evolving Complex Relationships 20

    Christi's Story 21

    Shella's Story 22

    Can You Afford to Be a "Sandwich Generation" Caregiver? 22

    Gayle's Story 23

    Martha's Story 24

Chapter 5: The Shadow Caregiving Economy 26

    Unpaid Care 26

    Thinking of Self-Funding? 27

    Tom's Story 28

    Home Sweet Home 28

    We Can Depend on Our Friends 29

    Adrianna's Story 29

Recognizing Alzheimer's...30
Elnora's Story 30

Chapter 6: Publicly Funded Long-Term Care Landscape....................33
Federal Efforts...33
State Efforts..34

Chapter 7: Caregiving Changes Everything...37
Paul's Story 37

Chapter 8: Are You Jodi? 39
Jodi's Story 40

Section II 42

Practical but Flexible Approaches to Overcoming Planning Challenges and Objections 43

Chapter 9: Overcome Challenges and Objections 44
I Haven't Really Focused on It! 44
Busy with Life and Competing Priorities.......................................45
Uncomfortable Giving Up Control 48
Unwilling to Share Personal Information 50
Inadequate or Miscalculated Longevity or Retirement Planning....... 52
Diminished Physical or Mental Capacity 53
Dismissing or Ignoring Reality 55
Excuses Not to Participate 56
Don't See the Need 58
We Need a Family Tracking/Communication Tool...........................60
Unsure Who to Include in the Care Squad or CPT? 61
It's Too Much Work!...62
This Doesn't Align with Our Cultural Norms...................................64
Unrealistic Expectations of Family Members 65
Too Much Family Conflict 65
Doing Too Much...67
Denial and Optimism Bias 69
Longevity Literacy...69
Medicare Confusion..70
Unsure How to Ask Unpaid People to Help 72
Unsure How to Hire Paid Help?..72
Someone feels that they live too far away to participate...................75
All the Funding Options Feel Unaffordable.....................................76

Where's the Money Coming From? 76
My Parent is Uninsurable.. 78
I Am Confused about the Types of Insurance.................................... 79

Chapter 10: Concluding Thoughts and Encouragement........................ 81

Section III 83

APPENDIX A: Care Guide Content List.. 84
Care Guide App 84
Basic Legal Documents 85
Personal Contact Information 86
Professional Contact Information 87
Financial Worksheet 87
Personal Documents... 88
Business Documents 89

APPENDIX B: Funding Sources and Planning Options 90
For those in good or relatively good health: 90
For those with some health issues or budget concerns: 90
For those who meet the definition of impoverished: 91
For many, but not all:... 91

APPENDIX C: Resource Links 92
Cost-of-Care sites: 92
Social Security sites:.. 92
Caregiver Advice, Support, and Resources 93
Additional Resources 95

About the Author 97

Introduction

Our longer lives seems to be increasingly impacted by change but caring for one another is a constant. It is a part of the continuum of life. Every generation will include caregivers. I have spent a couple of decades trying to find the "words" and a "roadmap" to help individuals and families prepare to navigate and plan for this phase of life. My passion comes from both professional exposure to the societal challenges of caregiving and from personal experience.

Fortunately, my family planned in advance for when my mother might need extended care. My sisters and I all lived in different states when we got a call from my mom saying she had been diagnosed with a debilitating disease. We were devastated. Although never an easy situation, not having to decide about the affordability of care options, legal, and personal responsibilities greatly reduced the stress and family discord. We concentrated on spending time with my mother and pulled *together* as a family. This experience inspired my sisters and I to plan for the possibility of our own extended care needs.

Unfortunately, the family situation into which I remarried proved more challenging. My in-laws had a family history of both Alzheimer's disease and longevity. While advances in medicine and science continue to extend how long we may live, treatment for diseases of the brain has seen only marginal improvements. Knowing the gene for Alzheimer's disease can be inherited overshadowed family care planning conversations. Sadly, the lack of planning and inclusiveness had a very negative impact on my new family's finances and emotional cohesiveness. Discourse and disagreements about planning led to no planning. When my mother-in-law needed care, even minor decisions led to misplaced anger and nasty commentary, which was very upsetting for her. It was a harsh lesson that helped me develop a three step planning roadmap since unspoken or unresolved issues become communication stoppers.

My mother-in-law's generation traditionally cared for their parents and didn't face many of the physical, psychological, and financial challenges of today's mobile, dual-income, and complex living arrangements. Billions are spent on anti-aging advertising and products. At any age, when approached about planning for older ages, many individuals feel it dismisses them as active contributors, making their long life feel more like an inconvenience than a gift. In a youth-oriented society like ours, discussing aging and the care needs associated with declining health or mental awareness is often a taboo topic.

Of the two books I authored, one directed at industry professionals and the other at consumers, I am pleased to share that the latter, *How Not To Pull Your Family Apart: A Practical Guide to Caregiving and Financial Stability* became an Amazon bestseller in three categories. I am thrilled to know that the three step roadmap in the book was helpful in starting and continuing conversations that led to some successful planning. On the other hand, other readers shared with me that objections and challenges blocked their success. What bothers me most is that many of us are unfamiliar with the evolving needs or personal dynamics involved in extended or LTC—until it's too late. Few have the knowledge or experience to create an organized approach. As a result, individuals, families, and professionals shy away from the discussion for fear of insulting or upsetting someone. Those brave enough to bring forward the need to plan are often met with abrupt or offensive refusals to share information. The lack of a plan can tear a caregiver's life apart.

Aside from my experience and research, to make sure I was not just limiting myself to information and stories shared by family and friends, I consulted with individuals and financial professionals to gather tips and ideas. It is my sincere hope that this book will help families overcome objections that relegate extended care planning to stressful crisis planning.

How to Use This Book

You only have two choices when it comes to caregiving: plan or panic. Talking about planning for extended or LTC is difficult. Caregiving is complex. Using a system or roadmap to guide the process is an effective approach to move the conversation from a discussion to an action plan. I want to share my three-step approach with you. It is flexible enough to be personalized, but well-organized to ensure an extended care plan emerges.

To facilitate using the three steps, this book includes suggested responses to various challenges and objections that you may encounter. The suggestions constitute simple, practical responses that will help you to craft critical conversations so that you and someone you love are prepared instead of confused and panicked when extended care is needed.

Shadow Caregiving System: The What, Who, When, Why, and How

What is the Shadow Caregiving System/Economy?

In the U.S., caregivers account for more than ninety-five percent of informal care. I refer to it as the shadow caregiving system, since it is not a formerly organized or government supported system. However, it is a very important and essential system.

This book is about you! You probably don't even see yourself as a caregiver or think about what will happen if you are called upon to be a caregiver. You are or will do what needs to be done. You will carry on with no real training or knowledge about the vast body of available support, services, options, and programs to help a loved one plan in advance, support them during, or deal with the crisis stage in their caregiving journey. You are or will be a typical caregiver participant in the shadow caregiving system and contribute to the shadow caregiving economy.

Being a caregiver is a juggling act. It's a bumpy road with changes and unpredictable incidents which may be exacerbated by erratic interactions with friends and family. As you read about the shadow caregiving system/economy, you will see that planning for extended care, without guidance, is really difficult. However, not dealing with being unprepared is worse and results in uncontrolled and unwanted physical, psychological, and financial costs.

Who else is concerned about the coming tsunami of care needs?

Our current national caregiving system is dysfunctional and has contributed to the formation of the shadow caregiving system. Understaffing, underfunding, a lack of coordinated services, supports, and public education has resulted in individuals and families finding themselves unprepared for the costs associated with caregiving and thus joining the ranks of the shadow caregiving economy. After Medicaid, personal funds are the biggest contributor to caring for loved ones.

- Government Legislation, Initiatives, Task Forces, Studies, and Programs

The lack of preparation for the demographic aging of Americans has broad implications. America's lack of LTC education, coordination of services, supports, and funding impacts the federal government and individual states. The current and evolving approaches to individual, state, and federal LTC planning may affect you long before you need long-term care.

- Insurance Carriers and Vendors

Insurance carriers continue to create and sell products that respond to current and future care costs and care needs. They recognize the need for a wide variety of insurance and non-insurance products that are personalized according to health, age, living arrangements, budgets, etc.

- Technology

Innovative 24/7 applications and devices responsive to various phases of the extended and LTC journey are available. Whether it's a device to keep someone at home for a longer period, an alert about an abuse, a scam, a change in schedule payments, or to help organize and assure the privacy of the Care Guide, "there's an app for that!"

- Individual and Family Planning

The demands brought on by longevity has many implications. The lack of financial education along with the shortage of supports and resources means more of us have to find our own path for extended care planning. Hopefully, my three-step roadmap will help you figure out what works for you and those you care about.

When do you need to start?

Now! Chances are you are busy living life. Chances are you don't live next door to your parents or someone who will depend on you, even if they think they won't depend on you. If you live more than thirty minutes away from your family (no matter how you define family), you are considered a long-distance caregiver. Chances are when you suggest discussing and planning for potential caregiving needs, you will get shut down or get a flat "no thanks" response. However, every year that you wait, options become more limited and housing and funding options may become more expensive or unaffordable. You want to start early, so it's a conversation and not a disaster. Some of my suggestions on crafting critical conversations will help to get you where you need to be.

Why do you need a three step roadmap to achieve your goal?

Planning for future care is a challenge. In many cases, there are valid competing priorities that seem to take precedence over planning for future care. As you will see below, the three steps offer a strategy that gradually builds to a personalized stable plan. Step one, the Care Guide, privately/securely compiles all sorts of past and present information. Step two, the Care Squad, is a practical approach to expanding the care recipient's/caregiver's pool of support. Step three, the Care Planning Team, creates an inclusive education team who discover there are many options/resources that fit different budgets, care needs, and living arrangements. Planning for extended care isn't something you can google and be done with it! Go from "why didn't we?" to "we are making some real progress!"

How do you effectively deal with objections and challenges?

To get unwilling family members to discuss this sensitive topic, conversations can't result in someone feeling offended, angry, or that you are inserting yourself into their private affairs. Use the suggested critical conversation responses in Section II, in conjunction with one or all of the three steps to move from silence, stubbornness, fear, or sadness to constructive planning conversations. Plan, don't panic!

Section I

Chapter 1

What's in a Name

It is worth reviewing some basic terminology. The terms long-term care (LTC) and long-term services and supports (LTSS) cover a range of services provided to people with long-term physical or cognitive limitations. The private insurance industry typically uses LTC or extended care as a shorthand term, while government, academic, and public policy literature typically use LTSS.

It is also important to recognize that different cultures and organizations use different terminology to describe the role of a person who supports another person's needs. The term caregiver is popular. Others prefer to use terms like care partner, caretaker, or they simply lack a formal term all together. Family, in this book, is used in the broadest possible sense to include spouses, partners, siblings, friends, community, cousins, tribes, nieces, nephews, grandparents, parents, godparents, and others. They are the backbone of the shadow caregiving system.

Commonly, LTC does not typically refer to medical care, but rather assistance with some basic personal tasks of everyday living. You may also hear the term, activities of daily living (ADL), which is commonly used to determine if an individual's needs qualify them for government LTC assistance or insurance benefits. If you think of what you do when you wake up in the morning, it may help you to remember the six most common ADLs. You (#1) transfer (get out of bed/chair), you may deal with (#2) incontinence, or (#3) toileting, you may (#4) bathe or shower, get (#5) dressed, and (#6) eat. Alternatively, cognitive impairment is another qualifying event for triggering benefits. Cognitive impairment is when a person has trouble remembering, learning new things, concentrating, or making decisions that affect their everyday life. Alzheimer's disease is an example of cognitive impairment.

Chapter 2

A Three Step Roadmap

We're going to be talking a lot about my three-step roadmap throughout this book, so let's summarize what these steps are and how they help you formulate an extended care plan. Once you select your approach, we will look at some practical but flexible responses to objections or challenges you may encounter.

Step One: Care Guide: The "I Care and Respect You"

Conversation

The Care Guide is a living document that should be created for every member of the family. It reduces stress by consolidating and organizing crucial, hard to locate and up-to-date information such as past and current health details, professional and personal contact information, financial and retirement worksheets, personal wishes, thoughts, letters, photos, legal documents, health insurance or government programs, passwords, final arrangements or end-of-life wishes, etc.

One of my clients, an only child, told me her father refused to share personal information with anyone. Her mother passed away, and she knew she would be his caregiver. I suggested that both of them create a Care Guide. She explained to her father why he might need her personal information and she might need his. Neither would have to make decisions for the other or search through their stuff—a real invasion of privacy. Using an app that unlocks information as specific triggers occur would satisfy their need to keep information private, but also satisfy the need to access information when necessary. After filling in some basic information, as they had doctor appointments, used passwords, or noted missing documents suggested by the Care Guide list, they each could continue to fill in the blanks. Please refer to Appendix A for a helpful list of information to personalized your Care Guide.

Step Two: Care Squad: The "What If" Conversation

The objective of the Care Squad is to create a process for family and friends to react cooperatively when care needs evolve or emergencies arise. When my mother-in-law needed care, it led to such chaos that she told me she felt helpless and guilty to be the cause of so much stress. That sad experience led me to create step two, the Care Squad.

The squad creates an action plan. It assigns each person a role. A simple list or chart indicating the responsibility and the person's name works well. Who calls the doctor or ambulance? Who's in charge of handling the bills or interacting with insurers? Who contacts other family members or friends? You get the idea. When there is a tense situation, those with a role or responsibility act, while others act out.

Step Three: Care Planning Team: The "Discovery" Conversation

Caregiving doesn't happen in a vacuum. According to a 2023 AARP Public Policy Institute report, family caregivers provided an estimated thirty-six billion hours of unpaid care—estimated to be worth six hundred billion dollars. That's the current estimated composition of the shadow caregiving system/economy, and it's growing!

As a nation, we need to stop pushing this issue to the back burner. There are simply not enough trained caregivers and staff to take care of everyone who will need assistance. More and more of us will be obliged to take on a role for which few of us are trained. The objective of Care Planning Team (CPT) members is to learn about and discuss limited and extended care planning options without a sales pitch or pressure. Multi-generational CPTs offer the best mix of ideas, tools, technology, and support. You may want to invite professionals, guest specialists, or access recorded videos to learn about different planning options. Please refer to Appendix B for some options and information to kick-off your CPT.

Chapter 3

A Bumpy Journey

Caregivers and care recipients are on a unique journey together with many twists and turns, lasting a few days to a few decades when someone's physical or mental abilities are in decline. Consequences along the journey can be emotionally, physically, and financially taxing as things escalate on many fronts. A friend of mine described her bumpy caregiving journey.

A Friend's Story

Some days, I feel like the only thing my mother and I can agree on is that we disagree. When I turn to family members and friends for support, I overwhelm them with my anger and frustration. I either wind up wasting their time with excessive complaining or I don't really engage at all. Sometimes, their helpful suggestions make me feel humiliated or ashamed that I'm not handling things better.

Smoothing out the bumps, one step at a time

I told my friend to begin with identifying things that take her and her mother onto common ground. No matter how narrow that might be; it will create a shared reality. The objective of finding common ground is to transfer the focus from the two of you to someone or something unrelated to the two of you. The underlying tension is still there, but focusing on common ground allows for a conversation that directs attention away from personal judgments.

Lyndsay's Story

My friend, Lyndsey, was visiting her grandparents. Her grandfather asked her to explain something in his billing statement. His 2023 statement included a charge of $250 that he didn't recognize. She said that they were both "totally amazed" at the charge. This created a common ground conversation to discuss fraud without saying "elder fraud." This led to asking what the plan going forward would look like. "Not sure" was the response. Lyndsey suggested creating a Care Squad with Lyndsey in charge of helping her grandfather with medical billing correspondence. The Care Squad grew from there and their next step was the Care Guide!

Chapter 4

Caregivers Are Us

Although many of us don't self-identify as caregivers, we are active members of the shadow caregiving system, with one out of every five American adults, from all walks of life and backgrounds, providing care in a given year.

Are you a participant in the Shadow Caregiver System?

According to an AARP study, *Caregiving in the U.S. 2020*, the generational makeup of the shadow caregiving system is shifting. In a few short years, from 2015 to 2020, caregiving responsibilities shifted away from both the Silent/Greatest Generation (born 1945 or prior) and Baby Boomers (born 1946-1964) to Generation X (born 1964 to 1980), Millennials (born from 1981 to 1996), and Generation Z (born 1997 or after).

Evolving Complex Relationships

The shadow caregiving system is complex. What category do you see yourself in of those listed below? In today's society, there are many different types of relationships that result in various caregiving implications and complications:

- Heterosexual or same sex
- Committed but not legally married
- Long-term marriages
- Short-term marriages
- International marriages
- Single income and dual income
- Children or no children
- Re-marriages and step-children
- Solo-agers

Even in the case of long-term marriages, where there may be only one set of parents for each partner, Baby Boomers are more likely to be alone in their later years, whether divorced, widowed, or never married. There was a decrease in the number of children Boomers had compared to previous generations, thus shrinking the caregiver pool. Being both less likely to have a spouse and to have fewer adult children, one in four Boomers is at risk of becoming an elder orphan or solo-ager. If your parent, relative, or close friend fall into this category, they may rely more heavily on you. Without a plan, you could find yourself with increased emotional and physical strain, competing demands of work and caregiving, as well as financial hardships.

At the opposite end of the spectrum are remarriages with a potentially bigger caregiving pool, especially if there are combined households with multiple children, step-children, parents, and grandparents. That translates into multiple but complicated caregiving obligations and expenses. International marriages and same-sex marriages may present legal, distance, or contract snags. Whether due to a lack of available or connected caregivers, financial preparedness, or medical and staffing shortages, caregiving responsibilities may become your unexpected, if not unmanageable, obligation.

Christi's Story

Christi's dad called her to say that her mom's scoliosis was worsening. He now had to do many of the things she once did, but can no longer handle. He was trying (and newly appreciative of how much she managed) but he simply could not keep up. It was starting to impact his own health. Christi lives in Italy (her husband is stationed there) and has two sisters stateside. Only one sister lives close enough to be of assistance. Christi, her sisters, and her dad got on a zoom call and used the three steps to create a plan. Christi's Care Squad assignment is to handle the bank accounts which she can do electronically while in Italy, her out-of-state sister will do the research on care services and supports, and the sister living close by will help with laundry, shopping, and meal prep. In this way, the Care Squad created a practical and guilt-free zone for each family member!

Shella's Story

It is important to think about who might hope or expect you to be their caregiver. My client, Shella, told me her daughter would be her caregiver. Her daughter thought so as well. That was the plan. However, Shella's husband is an only child. When his mother, quickly followed by his father, needed care, Shella stepped up and helped, although it took a toll on her since his parents didn't have a Care Guide. It was stressful. Her sick mother-in-law's responses were not reliable. In the middle of handling care for her husband's parents, her mother had a mild stroke and needed her help. You can imagine the rest of the story.

Can You Afford to Be a "Sandwich Generation" Caregiver?

There are now four generations of caregivers in the workplace. According to key findings in a recent *AgeWave Report*, eighty-one percent of caregivers are employed part time and sixty-four percent are employed full time. Complicating matters further, many of us are also now caught in the sandwich generation syndrome, which is defined as those caregivers who are simultaneously raising children while caregiving for aging parents or grandparents. Just under fifty percent of caregivers fall into this category. Will you add to that number?

Gayle's Story

> I was visiting with my son. His neighbor, Gayle, stopped by to drop off her children. Kaisha is a schoolmate of my son's youngest daughter. Gayle's son, Colton, is eight years old. Colton was not happy about the drop, but Gayle needed to handle the ongoing extended care needs of her father which didn't stop just because it was a weekend and the kids were home. Gayle also confided to my son that she's afraid she'll lose her job because between her dad duties and children's needs, she is physically at work but mentally absent.

Women, like Gayle, are most likely to take on the role of caregiver. Much of the caregiving is shifting to Gen X women in their fifties whose careers are shortened or negatively impacted by eldercare, resulting, during their earning years, of an average loss of $300,000 in lost earnings and savings.

Gayle is typical of many Gen Xers. According to the Society of Actuaries, senior members of Generation X are staring down at a potentially acute financial crunch-even without caregiving complications. They are in a different situation than the generation before them (Baby Boomers). They face higher student loan debt, have less access to defined benefit plans, and many don't have the financial ability to save for retirement. They don't have any cushion to absorb unplanned or unfunded family caregiving needs.

It doesn't look as if it will be any easier if you are a Millennial. A Goldman Sachs report found that seventy percent of Millennials expect caregiving to undermine their progress toward retirement goals. Additionally, seventy-two percent predict they will lose earnings and career momentum due to caregiving.

Martha's Story

My daughter shared with me that one of her friends, Martha, a Millennial, told her that her family has "voluntold" her to take on the caregiving duties of her grandparents. Her parents are saving hard for their retirement and are concerned about remaining independent as they age. They believe their daughter, a

Millennial, has more time than them to make up for the loss of income due to caregiving.

Martha is now part of the Millennial generation that has taken time away from work for caregiving, and as a result more than half paused saving for retirement or drew down their savings. Without a plan, caregiving has a multigeneration impact.

Chapter 5

The Shadow Caregiving Economy: The Rising Cost of Care

Unpaid Care

The fact is longevity and demographics play a significant role in the growth of the shadow caregiving system. The effect of those two realities literally figure into the increasing shadow caregiving economy. What do you need to know?

For over twenty years, about every five years, AARP has conducted a study which includes caregivers of all ages and ethnicities and addresses the impact caregiving is having on the lives of unpaid caregivers. In their new thirty-one-page report, *Valuing the Invaluable*, AARP paints a vivid picture of the current state of family caregiving in the United States. The organization's Public Policy Institute found that: "In 2021, about 38 million family caregivers in the United States provided an estimated 36 billion hours of care to an adult with limitations in daily activities. The estimated economic value of their unpaid contributions was approximately $600 billion." That's a mind-numbing number!

By 2034, AARP notes, "adults aged 65 and older will outnumber children under the age of 18 for the first time." This shift in available potential caregivers, along with a shortage of professional and non-professional staffing, will put added pressure on those in need of care and may force some to access state assistance programs. Furthermore, we are seeing a financial shortfall for some Medicaid and other state programs that may result in premium assessments from the paychecks of working individuals to fund a state run LTC program. Families will need to plan or become part of an unhappy statistic. And now you know why planning is a must have, not a nice to have!

Thinking of Self-Funding?

One of the responses that my colleagues and I often hear, in order to avoid a discussion about offsetting the cost of LTC, is "I'll self-insure." Since insurance is, by definition, a pooling of resources, that translates into a pooling of only *your* resources. Is that a solid plan? Are you insuring just yourself? Is your income adequate? Are your resources liquid?

Tom's Story

A friend of mine, Tom, is a very successful financial professional. One of his clients derives most of their income from his real estate business. During an investment plan review, he asked his client to indicate where the actual funds would come from if he needed extended care. Since current income would not cover the addition of extended care needs in the way the client envisioned, Tom asked him, "Which building are you going to sell first? Hopefully, it will be in a good sellers' market, so you're not pressured into a fire sale. Let's also consider if it will impact the loans, taxes, and other aspects of the business." After some thought, his client asked him for an alternative suggestion.

Regardless of your financial situation, you need to ask yourself if your pool includes adequate income or easily accessible liquid assets.

Home Sweet Home

Aging-in-place sounds ideal and inexpensive. But is it? If you haven't had a discussion with your potential care recipient, let's think this through. There are some real challenges.

First, will the home need modifications to accommodate aging-in-place? For example, let's say you live in a single unit home. Are all the rooms, including the bathroom, accessible without stairs and are doorways wide enough for maneuvering a wheelchair? Or maybe you live or relocated to an apartment building. Is there a ramp or elevator to help you into your apartment? If renovations are needed, are professionals and craftsmen available at the price and schedule that accommodates your care recipient's needs?

We Can Depend on Our Friends

Adrianna's Story

Adrianna, an acquaintance of mine, shared her story with me. Her family had never discussed the topic of extended care planning, so there was no plan when her dad had a stroke. Since her mother didn't want to ask Adrianna to give up her job and her own family routine to help with her dad, she suggested they ask someone from their faith community to come in and help. There were several that offered to drop off food (not that her picky husband would eat it!) or help lift him out of bed and help shower him (although neither she nor Adrianna thought that he would be comfortable with that arrangement!). Forced to hire someone, Adrianna's mom hoped to find someone pretty easily. Aside from the well-documented staffing shortage, Adrianna explained that hiring someone entailed a background check, a contract, payroll, and scheduled tax withholding and filing, having a backup replacement, and so on. Her mom became very stressed and upset. So did Adrianna, who was sorry they had never discussed the possibility of her dad needing help!

It's not an uncommon story. You don't know what you don't know. What you do know is that the sooner you use any or all of my three steps the better, since conversations become more difficult as time goes by.

Recognizing Alzheimer's

Elnora's Story

Once, while visiting my mother, her neighbor Elnora stopped over. She knows that I work in the extended care planning field. I know she works full time and loves her job. She surprised me by telling me that she was at the end of her rope. With her mother's declining health, she found in-home help to take over some of her caregiving responsibilities, but it's turned into a nightmare. Her mother continually gets rid of the help! Either she's rude, offensive, and uncooperative, or she screams and cries to give the impression they're hurting her. Either way, they quit. With the staffing shortage, it's easy for them to find work elsewhere, leaving Elnora unable to convince them to stay on.

If Elnora has the budget, she'll be forced to hire an agency to find qualified help who understands and has experience with clients like her mother. She may incur an agency fee in addition to the caregiver's fee. Additionally, agencies generally require minimum hours per visit as well as travel and other expenses. The rapid increase in the cost of hiring help can be an unpleasant surprise for those who haven't investigated it.

Elnora would benefit from education and a frank discussion about what is happening with her mother. But, as is very common, both she and her mother have avoided acknowledging her mother's deteriorating mental capacities. The lack of a plan is wreaking havoc with their lives. Ultimately, a television commercial made her realize she had to acknowledge and deal with the real issue. The infomercial addressed the realities of caring for someone with Alzheimer's disease. It showed mature hands with a voiceover that sounded like a daughter announcing, "these hands used to hold me as a little girl and comfort me but now they have become aggressive." The words hitting, pushing, throwing things appeared on the screen. Then, there was an image of the mouth of the mature adult with a voiceover saying, "these lips used to sing me lullabies but now they have become unrecognizable." The words cursing, shouting, and spitting then appeared on the screen. This disturbing but honest message from the Alzheimer's organization suggested that Elnora's mother could have Agitation In Alzheimer's disease. The ad ended with the words, "Help your loved one. Learn more at AgitationInAlz.com." Learn and plan.

Chapter 6

The Emerging Publicly Funded Long-Term Care Landscape

Individuals and families are not the only ones impacted by the increasing cost of care. Given the aging demographic in America, federal and states budgets can expect an increase in Medicaid recipients resulting in a growing financial shortfall.

Federal Efforts

For more than thirty years, federal policymakers have put forward a variety LTSS proposals. Most of the proposals never made it out of Congress. The Affordable Care Act of 2010 established the

Community Living Assistance Services and Supports (CLASS) Plan, but was subsequently repealed in 2013.

In response to the Biden administration's April 2023 Executive Order 14025, the Centers for Medicare and Medicaid Services (CMS) is accepting letters of interest for a test model, Guiding an Improved Dementia Experience (GUIDE). According to the order, GUIDE aims to be "an innovative new health care payment and service delivery model focused on dementia care that would include family caregiver support such as respite care." The model will focus on dementia care management and aims to improve quality of life for people living with dementia, reduce strain on their unpaid caregivers, and enable people living with dementia to remain in their homes and communities. It hopes to achieve these goals through a comprehensive package of care coordination and care management, caregiver education and support, and respite services. The model is scheduled to run for eight years beginning July 1, 2024.

State Efforts

State Medicaid budgets are the dominant source of payment for long-term care, followed by out-of-pocket payments by individuals and families. In response to the rising costs of hospital and facility care, some states authorize programs for qualified beneficiaries to access in-home LTSS.

The increasing cost-of-care incurred by Medicaid state budgets does not appear to be sustainable. Individual states are in various stages of tackling the growing needs and resulting expenditures for our older and disabled population. More and more states are actively engaged in proposing legislation, creating a task force, a study, or funding for a study, etc.

State LTC legislation trends include:

- Tax and Incentives
- Publicly funded LTC programs
- Rate regulation
- Product innovation
- Consumer Education

In 2019, the State of Washington enacted legislation for a publicly funded LTC program. On July 1, 2023, the WA Cares Fund began collecting premium assessments from employees who work in the state. Income from W-2 salaries are not capped and include bonuses, commissions, stock options, etc. Once a claimant is approved for benefits, the claimant will have access to $36,500 (in the future, this amount can be adjusted for inflation). Many months of work went into designing the program. Efforts to work through many challenging program details and the needs of Washingtonians are ongoing. Many Washingtonians purchased private LTC insurance to avoid the premium assessment and have more control of their care options.

As of this writing, there are over 20 states in some stage of looking into a publicly funded LTC, better coordination of services and supports, and/or consumer education programs. In some cases, a state program may be a good option, but you need to understand what it offers and what falls on you, the caregiver, to manage. Since many private options depend on health status and cost increases with age, now is the time to start the discussion and discover what will work for you. That is the objective of the Care Planning Team.

Chapter 7

Caregiving Changes Everything

You probably don't have a clear idea if someone will need care until they actually do. Understanding the impact that their care needs may have on your life doesn't mean you won't be a good caregiver when the call comes, it just means you should seriously consider creating a plan now to help avoid many of the negative consequences that a lack of planning can entail.

Paul's Story

A client of mine, Paul, is single and on a good career path at his firm. He approached his parents about planning for short-term or extended care. He was told to back off. His dad was very firm, saying that as the head of household, "I have everything under control." He said Paul would find out about the plan in the unlikely event that they would need his help. A couple of years later, I got a call from him. His dad had suffered a debilitating stroke, leaving him unable to effectively communicate. His mother knew nothing about the plan. It makes you think about people who equate silence and stonewalling with control. Paul is now spending his time sorting through all kinds of personal and business information, limited by missing documents and passwords while trying to help his mother manage his father's bills and overall finances. On top of all of that, his dad is frustrated and resents the way things are being handled. If only he had shared his plan, assuming he had one! Now Paul worries about his parents, finances, and the long range impact on his health and career.

In a recent *AgingCare.com* survey, caregivers reported that the cost of caring for a parent has impacted their ability to plan for their future. In an AARP study, *Caregiving in the U.S.*, caregivers reported significantly worse health across all ages, among both low- and high-income caregivers, among all marital statuses, and among both those who had a choice and those who had no choice in providing care. This isn't an experience you want for your family, no matter the make-up of your family circle.

Chapter 8

Are You Jodi?

Hopefully, you are now convinced that you need to acknowledge both the joys and the responsibilities that come with the potential for longevity and changes in life stages. Starting early and incorporating conversations with family members can center around birthdays, anniversaries, milestones, celebrations, or traditional holidays. If you wait for a scary, sad, or upsetting crisis to push everyone into action, the situation will be tense and upsetting. It will be too late to avoid some of the worst consequences of delayed planning.

Sometimes it's the caregiver who doesn't recognize what's happening. In the excerpt below from my second book, *How Not To Pull Your Family Apart*, the main character, Jodi, gets a wake-up call. Once Jodi realizes what caregiving is doing to her life, she is willing to discuss a plan for her parent's care.

Jodi's Story

It's been a gradual process. As a result, Jodi doesn't really even associate all she is doing with caregiving. Jodi's husband and two children worry about the toll it's taking on her. Sleep deprivation, unhealthy eating habits, a lack of exercise, a lack of time to spend with friends or her grandchild are just a few of the signs of her stress and overburdened schedule. Her children suspect that Jodi didn't take or wasn't offered a promotion she had been working towards due to spending increasingly more time and attention to her parent's needs. As we already learned, family caregivers who disrupt their careers or leave the labor force entirely to meet caregiving demands can face substantial economic risk leading to short-and long-term financial impacts. Jodi's children, Erik and Nicole, finally approach their dad since their mom quickly brushes off their attempts to discuss the situation. They are unsure how to start the conversation without upsetting both Jodi and their grandparents. They decide to give her a third-party planning journal article. Fortunately, she self-identifies with some of the consequences of caregiving and why the family is concerned. Without a conversation, there is no planning.

Section II

Practical but Flexible Approaches to Overcoming Planning Challenges and Objections

The three steps guide you in creating a Care Guide, a Care Squad, and a Care Planning Team. The steps offer a roadmap that leads to an extended care plan. In my experience, unfortunately, many readers and professional acquaintances encounter objections to planning for something they consider to be far into the future. However, plans for extended care do not come together overnight. No one is asking you to buy anything today. Still, you absolutely must make the time to discuss protecting yourself and your loved ones from the risks, expenses, and personal burdens of unforeseen and unplanned extended care needs.

This section offers potential responses to common objections and challenges which coordinate with each of the three steps.

Chapter 9

Overcome Challenges and Objections

If you ask three people for advice, you are likely to get three different answers. Equally, there are many responses to challenges and objections. To be the best family in the history of ever, you need to use or modify whichever of these practical suggestions work for you.

I Haven't Really Focused on It!

And that's the truth!

- Prioritizing what's important to us differs not only by age and genre but also by our personal life story. Turning an intangible future scenario into a tangible plan is a gradual process. Often we aren't sure what we want because we don't ask ourselves or life events change things without our input. So, when you ask a parent or friend what their plan looks like, don't be shocked that they honestly don't know. Ask if one of their friends is going through a long-term care event or has moved into an assisted living facility. It might get them talking.

Busy with Life and Competing Priorities

Competing priorities can push planning for future needs to the bottom of the list. They say if you want something done, ask a busy person. Families can tag someone to take control and use the three-step roadmap to organize a more inclusive family care plan.

Liliana's Story

Liliana takes control despite having two sisters and a brother. Her mother is a widow who assumes her children will care for her when she gets older. Liliana is a nurse, so her siblings see her in the caregiver role. She wants them to understand that she will handle certain aspects of parental care, but she has a job and family to consider. Liliana uses the three steps to get her siblings more involved. "Mom is starting to show signs of slowing down and losing interest in participating in events. We need to recognize that she isn't well. We can anticipate that there will be several visits to the doctor,

45

imaging facilities, and a team of people who expect us to provide her medical history and appropriate documents. We need to fill out this Care Guide. I will handle that step. Next is the Care Squad. Mom is frightened and seeing we are organized will help her. If she needs surgery, after she returns home, there will be doctor visits, pharmaceutical and device pickups, shopping and meal prep, physical therapy, cleaning, laundry, and errands. We three need to divide up those duties and establish a schedule so no one is overwhelmed and Mom has proper care." After seeing her sisters and brother reluctantly nod their agreement, she continues, "Together we need to form a Care Planning Team. We are all busy and we need to find out what is available to help us help Mom!"

- Children and parents with busy lives often push off the "talk". As a result, planned or unplanned, children find themselves participating in the shadow caregiving system/economy. At the next opportunity, start with a general discussion about how the price for everything and anything is increasing. Rising healthcare costs are in the news and digging into our budgets. Let that reality create a CPT to review current and future extended care costs and a funding plan. (See Appendix C for links to cost of care sites.)

- Commercials, advertisements, and pop-ups seem to have a product or prescription for all kinds of aliments and illnesses for all ages and health conditions. As we suggested in Lyndsey's story, they provide a good jumping off point for common ground discussions about planning for longevity.

- Don't wait to own a crisis story! If a healthy parent lands in the hospital along with the care recipient that they were lifting out of bed or helping out of a shower, you'll own an expensive first-hand story. Crisis planning will then be your only option. (See Appendix C for a link about crisis planning.)

- Try a passive self-identification approach. Stories, like the ones included in this book, in the news, or shared by friends and families provide everyone with an opportunity to self-identify with some aspect of it. Isn't better to use a roadmap and discover options to avoid adding more to already busy schedules?

Uncomfortable Giving Up Control

Parents who pride themselves as being independent may refuse to include their children in the planning process.

- Take what you can get! Your parents may be willing to share the name and contact information of their advisor or whomever knows their plan. Make sure the parent has discussed with the trusted advisor or friend who should have access to which information.
- For parents who don't have a plan, challenging them to share what they don't have will probably backfire. Instead, ask them to join *your* CPT and include solutions that might work for them. (See Appendix B.)
- Send out a six-month schedule for in-person or virtual CPT meetings. Scheduling in advance sends two messages: one, this is our planning window before we don't have one and two, it's about working together and not seizing control.
- Offer the independent parent the three-step formula and suggest they talk about it with their friends. They may even lead a CPT group and create a plan without direct family involvement.
- Plan to leave control in *their* hands. Ask them to fill out a basic Care Guide (see Appendix A) with instructions, then

seal it and write on the front of the envelope: full name, address, date of birth, emergency designee, and name and phone number of the primary care physician. Be sure it is kept somewhere to which you have access. Better yet, suggest an electronic app with built-in controls. (See Appendix C.)

- Frame the conversation to include your understanding of their need to stay in control. You are creating a dialogue of what they want and not what you will do to or for them. Ask how family support or knowledge could insure they stay in control. Start rowing in the same direction!

- Insistence on staying in control may indicate they are hiding something. Suspicious behavior and affordability issues should move planning up on the priority list. Increased types and the frequency of needing prescriptive and over-the-counter drugs is common as we age. But listen for over enthusiasm, overuse, or abuse!

- Today's heightened security and legality requirements provide another common ground way to craft the conversation. (See Appendix A)

Jonas's story

Jonas's dad flat out refused to discuss long-term care. Jonas reminisced about his grandfather, particularly about how the family rallied around him as he aged. Jonas told his dad he hoped he would have the same experience, but so many things had changed since then. During the conversation, Jonas pointed out how you could no longer just tell a physician or bank that this was what your parent wanted. You needed to have proof. His dad got the message!

Unwilling to Share Personal Information

Working towards a plan requires sharing personal information, which may feel intrusive.

- The concern for keeping personal information private is understandable and should be respected. Offer Paul's story as an example of how a conversation now about planning will later avoid an invasion of personal health and financial information. There is an excellent app (see Appendix A) that coordinates with the Care Guide and allows the owner to dictate when different categories of information will be shared and with whom (a built-in Care Squad). Alternately, you can go old school and seal it in an envelope that is kept in a designated place.

- Sometimes help seems like handling. Move the focus from solving their problem or need. Engaging in creating a family Care Guide or CPT project avoids singling out one person's personal information. It will, however, expose missing information and documents.

- The closer you get to planning for a time when a care recipient will be less independent, the scarier it gets. If you are too young to walk in those shoes or your family ignores the effects of the passage of time, trust me, it's a conversation stopper. Try getting in tune with how a care recipient might approach planning—straight ahead, around the edges, keeping a safe distance by talking about someone else's story, or using a third party they trust who you don't even know they knew. Keep your feelings to the side and place their approach front and center.

- Emphasize that the family history is to be treasured and the Care Guide documents the family traditions and health history for generations to come. Approach the Care Guide in the same way as family ancestry or family lore: record it now while it's available from living descendants as you gather firsthand accounts. Include stories, pictures, letters, memorabilia, thoughts, etc. To put contributors at ease, use an app that allows for sharing while keeping some components private. (See Appendix A.)

51

- Not everything can be found in medical records, and sometimes you have to speak with family members to know the real story and bridge an understanding of why they feel the way they do about planning for a long life. Being a good listener is a good start.

Inadequate or Miscalculated Longevity or Retirement Planning

Recently, the word longevity frequently appears in publications and communications. But the lack of planning for longevity must be a no blame zone.

- Historically, the emphasis on saving/investments was on accumulation, not decumulation. For Baby Boomers, what would happen if they outlived their resources or had to spend them on healthcare was not a major part of the retirement conversation. And although many are not without credentials or successful work careers, some feel ashamed or diminished by a looming care planning deficit due to miscalculations or misplaced personal optimism. Admitting that they aren't adequately prepared is embarrassing and uncomfortable. Think about situations where you were ashamed or embarrassed and what you did to get over it. Apply that knowledge here.
- If you suspect a family member is embarrassed to discover the tables have turned and their child will need to parent them or

fund their needs, reinforce that it's a natural life stage in many cultures. It's an honor.

- People see you as less judgmental if you relate to their situation and present a positive attitude. Handle the situation by validating their feelings. It's a natural place to apply feel, felt, found. "I know how you feel; I have felt the same way myself, but you know what I found?"

Diminished Physical or Mental Capacity

- As we saw in Elnora's story, acknowledging diminishing mental capacity or mild cognitive impairment is often hidden or ignored. If your parent/spouse/partner is showing signs of physical or mental vulnerability, it is vital to get permissions early in the process. Professional medical help and legal documents provide support for both of you. (Refer to Appendix C.)
- Longevity is more than just a new buzz word when you consider the rising number of older people living long enough to experience mental incapacity. There is nothing to be ashamed about, just something to figure out. Discuss how treatments are evolving in the area of diseases of the brain. Meanwhile, create a Care Guide to record details before they are forgotten.

Establish a CPT to become educated about supportive organizations and care facility options.

- Old documents are just that, old. Make sure they are still valid. The Care Guide helps you to see what you may be missing. (See Appendix A.)

Lori's Story

Lori asked her mother if she had completed documents indicating who would be legally in charge of her finances if she couldn't handle it. Her mother answered, "Oh, Dad or you can handle things." Lori replied, "What! You think a doctor or you bank will just hand over control or decision making to one of us because we ask them to?" Lori's mom hadn't thought about the legalities of being able or unable to make decisions on her own. Not uncommon. Not a comfortable thought.

Whether through an elder care attorney, workplace benefit, or on-line service, several types of documents are a must. Working through the Care Guide to review and update even basic documents will bring up some holes in the planning process. For example, do you know the difference between a durable financial power of attorney and a health care power of attorney? There is an excellent book listed in Appendix C that's an easy read, but also highly educational.

Dismissing or Ignoring Reality

Ease into the reality of the scope and demands of providing extended or long-term care. Talk about the realities of a short-term care situation morphing into an extended care situation.

Erik's Story

Erik's dad needed a knee replacement. As a result of a complicated surgery, he wouldn't be able to comfortably walk for several months. He needed someone to help him up, help him with his personal hygiene, help him bathe (assuming he could step into the tub, sit down and get up, or was steady enough to shower), get undressed or dressed, shop and cook for him, carry his food for him since he was on crutches or wouldn't be steady enough to carry hot food for some time, drive him to doctor and physical therapist appointments, pick up or supervise his medications (including pain medication dosages), and other things. The care duties involved in a knee replacement are hopefully temporary. Ask yourselves, "As a busy family, are we prepared for temporarily care recipient's support, like for a knee replacement? What if temporary turns into extended or long-term care?"

- Select someone to take notes for those that miss CPT meetings, so they see formulating a plan by discovering options is a real undertaking and not just a casual gathering. If they dismiss you, move on without them.
- Ask who needs to limit their involvement in the CPT discovery process. Be realistic and work with those willing to participate. Ask if those who are unavailable would like to be periodically updated. As they see progress, it may increase their willingness to participate. On the other hand, if including them in updates creates stress and is counterproductive, limit their briefings to what has already been accomplished.

Excuses Not to Participate

You understand the need for planning and you want to organize a Care Squad but no one else wants to participate.

- Families come loaded with complex dynamics. After all, we spend years developing them. Don't start with "you are expected to help here." Leave negative, accusatory attitudes at the door. Instead, suggest roles for each person that they can handle. Be ready with basic roles for an immediate situation and more extensive roles as care becomes more extensive. For example, a basic role could be to start a phone chain to keep people up-to-date, while a more extensive role may include hospital, facility, or home visits. A role for someone living out of state could be to handle research or documentation.

- Create a dialogue instead of a mandate. Share or even critique someone else's family or friend's experience. Consider what went right and what could have been improved. Look for areas of agreement and flesh out those that will be more problematic.

- Avoid family discord. Hard as it may be, if someone opts to be left out, let it go. It's just a stressor you don't need. Find roles for everyone who wants to help. Fit the role to their availability and accessibility. For example, if someone doesn't live close by, their role can be to handle electronic billing. Someone else can handle communications with physicians or insurers. Someone coordinates a visitation schedule. You get the idea.

Don't See the Need

Why do we need an extended care plan? It's not a certainty and so far into the future. Use Care Squad "what if?" scenarios to envision the consequences of a lack of planning.

Paulo's Story

> Paulo's mother, the family's natural caregiver, unexpectedly passed away. It left a big hole in the family. Paulo's father wouldn't discuss someone else taking care of him. With his wife gone, when Paulo's dad did need care, he announced that he wanted to continue to age in the home he had shared with his wife. Despite his protests, his family felt the level of care needed was best provided in a facility. Aside from the emotional burden of moving his dad, there was the issue of funding his care.

- Imagine that your parent(s) want to move in with you. Do you have room? Will it be disruptive? Who will actually tend to their needs? Will you have to rely on government assistance?
- Envision various financial scenarios where you must provide the funding:

- o An extended or long-term care incident can directly affect cash flow. Without a funded plan, both caregiver and care recipient will unwillingly contribute to the growing shadow caregiving economy.
- o The illness may last long enough to require an invasion of capital (yours or theirs), which may result in unwanted tax consequences or unfortunate market timing and liquidity issues that further diminish resources or legacy plans.
- o In the case of spouses or siblings, every dollar used for care directly impacts the ability to generate income/savings. If care needs last a long time, it will impact the other family member's lifestyle and/or funding for their future care needs.
- o If a parent runs out of funds, they may qualify for government assistance or Medicaid. It is a complicated system. Are you prepared to help them understand the intricacies of applying? As their care needs change, do you understand how to work with the array of Long Term Services and Supports (LTSS) for both institutional care and home-and-community-based services (HCBS)?

    o   Accumulating funds takes time. A shortfall in funding future care needs can impact several generations, especially if one spouse or partner starts to exhaust funds intended for the couple. It can impact their retirement, force the healthy spouse to return to the workplace, or interfere with a child's career path.

The earlier you have these imaginary "what if?" conversations, the better.

We Need a Family Tracking/Communication Tool

There is a significant amount of information that needs to be chronicled and shared. We all lead busy lives and caregiving details get messy.

Steve's Story

After a fall, Steve and his brothers were expecting to admit their mother to an Assisted Living Facility, but when it finally happened, it all became very real. All the brothers are involved in her care. That's the good news! Keeping track of all the evolving details for her ongoing care and new living arrangement was another matter entirely. And, of course, there were all the additional facts, figures, and decisions involved in selling her home and its' contents. Using a single app, spreadsheet, or shared drive to collect and codify financial information is important to building and keeping family trust, transparency, and efficiency. It will save the brothers hours of work if the information is available and categorized as things unfold. It will also be very useful for an insurance, HSA reimbursement, or IRS audit. There is a timesaving app for that! (See Appendix C.)

Unsure Who to Include in the Care Squad or CPT?

Everyone gets to define their own version of family. In some cases, local community or faith-based Care Squad or CPT participants are like family.

- If a non-blood friend or neighbor will be involved, tell family members so they won't feel ignored or disrespected.
- Consider why using local help would or would not be better for the care recipient's safety and well-being. Perhaps they have lived in the town or neighborhood for many years and would be more, or perhaps less, comfortable using local services or faith-based support. As the Care Squad leader, you can work in a consultative role alongside other help.

- A member of the Care Planning team should become familiar with important details if government support, an organization, or care facility is in the plan to avoid surprises about costs, staffing, and evolving care treatments.
- If you are a solo-ager (a widow, divorcee, without children) at a minimum, you need a Care Guide, Care Squad, and a written plan.
- If you are married or in a committed relationship but only one of you can bear to discuss or plan for extended care, go ahead and get it done. After all, you tried and hit a wall. You need to build a bridge over that wall.

It's Too Much Work!

It feels like too much work with too much information to process.

- Make it fun!
  - Introduce some fun activities that are also educational. Engage the CPT member's natural curiosity. For example, use easy to access sites to estimate each member's longevity. (See Appendix C.)
  - Arrange the meetings around family events, meet-ups, or virtual calls where you bring your favorite drink or food.

- Make the work count!
  - Learn by introducing a jeopardy style game or quiz. For example, what do you think is the average number of years people use extended or long-term care services? How many days do you think Medicare will pay the full charges for a hospital stay? Does the government take care of extended care needs? Make sure you have a prize for the winner!
- Personalize the Work!
  - Consider obtaining estimates for funding future healthcare and consider the impact on everyone's retirement plan. Have your investment or workplace retirement plan advisor run the numbers? What is the effect of withdrawing different amounts of money at different times from your plan for extended care needs?
  - Access studies that list the best places to retire and why they made the list. Would your dream retirement place accommodate your envisioned extended care plan?
  - Engage an advisor or specialist to review the differences in the assisted living facilities (ALF) vs. continuing care retirement communities (CCRC) vs. aging-in-place. Do you know what you want? Can you afford it?
  - Have everyone contribute a statement or create a photo folder that shows family homes (or home modifications)

over the years that morphed along with their changing life stage. Suggest changes that may come into play over the next ten or twenty years.

This Doesn't Align with Our Cultural Norms

In some cultures or generations, discussing personal and sensitive topics, like planning for future care, may be viewed as disrespectful. The assumption is that it is the duty of family members to care for all family members. Make the exercise a positive and informational experience.

- Put the head of the family in charge of talking about the plan instead of having it as a discussion. At a minimum, the family will then know if there is a plan, what is expected of them, and how to plan for that responsibility.
- Offer a successful long-term care planning event or story about a family with a similar cultural orientation that celebrated their family plan.
- Have the head of the family create a personalized three-step guide. Include pictures and traditions to help future generations understand how the family cares for all its members.

Unrealistic Expectations of Family Members

What if your parents assume you are the plan?

- Whether you agree with their assumption or not, get ready. Reinforce that you are going to care for them but circumstances may dictate how that will unfold. You want to do the best job possible so start to plan early by exploring what is in place and what they will be entitled to access. Since actually needing care is often a disturbing thought, depersonalize it by talking about a temporary (injury or corrective surgery) or fictional case (Erik's story). It's much less frightening, but you get to understand what they assume will work, what you perceive is unlikely to work, and which supports or benefits you may need to explore.

Too Much Family Conflict

No two family members think alike, whether there are two or twenty members.

- There are situations where CPT members will not agree on a plan or where more than one member insists that their plan is best. Although not ideal, having a plan in place without full agreement is still better than no plan at all. The use of an outside fiduciary can be especially helpful when family members disagree or have been estranged from one another; engage a professional or a trusted neutral third party.

- Forming a CPT reinforces the importance of care coordination often included in LTC policies. For those who don't have this valuable benefit, the CPT can investigate public facsimiles like local area agency on aging that help you navigate what is available. (See Appendix C.)

- Sibling rivalry is real and when it is a question of caring for a loved one, it can become extreme. Remember, it must always be about what's best for the care recipient. Difficult as it is, emotions have to be controlled at some point. The fact that the care recipient will become more and more upset over the obvious rivalry should be the reason for parties to settle down, which may translate into using an advisor as a mediator. This is another reason why documents in the Care Guide are essential to establishing the decision maker.

- Dealing with other family members who may be over-or-under involved can create havoc. If you know from experience that this is what happens in your family, use a professional or faith-based advocate to create rules and parameters. Starting early is essential so the care recipient makes decisions and avoids a family war.

Doing Too Much

- This can occur in one of two ways:

  Either the caregiver suffers from a martyr or alpha child syndrome or no one will actually pitch in.

Jonathan's Story

I was having a quick coffee with a friend, Jonathan. He looked tense. He jumped when his cell phone buzzed, indicating a text. He groaned and explained that his mother was texting.

"It's every five minutes, and my sisters and brothers refuse to help."

"Why?" I asked.

"Because they want to do things their way and they always screw everything up."

I asked if he had tried to set up a plan so everyone knew how to help.

He took a sip of coffee and simply said, "No, I don't want them involved. I know what needs to be done and I'm better off without their interference."

I was confused since I heard a mixed message. Jonathan said they'd refused to help and then said that he didn't want their help.

Rosa's Story

Like so many caregivers, taking care of her father consumes most of Rosa's personal time and energy. When she tries to talk with her brother about their mother's growing dependency and her own exhaustion, her brother dismissed her. He accuses Rosa of exaggerating the situation. She tries to explain, but he shuts her down. As a result, she is in survival mode, operating as if everything is a ten. Rosa prioritizes caregiving over her own health care needs. She has delayed going to physical therapy for her hip discomfort, despite worsening pain. She skipped scheduling a colonoscopy despite her father dying of colorectal cancer. Rosa shows up to work looking exhausted. She has taken so much time off that her employer suggested she work only part-time.

When we think about our lifespan, we all hope to live a very long life. Rosa's lifespan may actually be shortened due to the intensity of caregiving she provides for her mother with no help from her brother. She is an example of when caregiving becomes the differential between life-span and health-span.

Denial and Optimism Bias

Two sides of the same coin.

- Some individuals will deny the possibility of ever needing long-term care. They insist they will do away with themselves if they ever do need extended or LTC. Start the conversation by agreeing that it is very unlikely that they will need care. Avoid any negative statistics or references to deteriorating health or mental capacity. Frame discussing a plan with the focus on assuring future comfort and control.
- The optimist believes their care needs are all taken care of. They are sure family will provide and government assistance is all they will need. Have them visit a Medicaid facility.

Longevity Literacy

"I don't know if I will live long enough to need extended care. So, why plan now?"

- This seems like a reasonable response. Along with a lack of financial literacy, there is also a lack of longevity literacy among the vast majority of U.S. adults. Spending time to discover your estimated longevity will create an awareness of potential later life care needs. Learning more about longevity helps all of us think about saving for retirement and, by extension, off-setting the risk of funding extended care. (Refer to Appendix C for links to estimate your projected longevity.)

Medicare Confusion

The parent or family believe that Medicare will pay for long-term care costs.

- It's a common misconception. The 2023 Medicare & You Handbook clearly states: "Some of the items and services basic Medicare doesn't cover include LTC (also called custodial care)."
- Relying on Medicare can leave a person requiring care with escalating costs to pay on their own. Without a plan of care, elderly are known to have skipped accessing some services due to cost concerns.

Margie's Story

A colleague of mine, Margie, is an experienced agent who offers long-term care insurance. Her mother often joined us when we got together. She was still a spry lady in her early 90's. A couple of years later, when she fell ill, Margie took her to the hospital where she stayed for several days. Margie was shocked when reviewing the bill she saw that the first 2 days of her mother's stay were not covered by Medicare. When she inquired, she was informed that the first two days were listed as "under observation" and not "admitted." Admitted means the patient is in the hospital under the care of a doctor, and under observation means the patient is staying in the hospital but as an outpatient. For the first two nights that her mother spent in the hospital, no admission papers had been signed, making her mom an under observation inpatient in the hospital. Her mother had to personally pay for those 2 days.

- Supplemental Plans: Medicare Advantage and Medicare Supplements only cover costs associated with Medicare.
- Medicaid is a program for the impoverished. Qualifying for Medicaid requires that the person meet very specific health and financial requirements. (See Appendix C for links to Medicare and Medicaid information).

Unsure How to Ask Unpaid People to Help

How do you frame a simple request for someone to be part of the Care Squad?

- You will need to have a detailed plan and the role to be fulfilled by someone you are asking to help. Work with their location, calendar, and schedule and be specific about your request. Remember to be practical, since, in some cases, time is of the essence and travel time can create a safety issue.
- Provide answers to questions they may or may not vocalize. What if I am away? What if I am the one who needs help? Will I be given instructions?
  How long will you need my help?

Unsure How to Hire Paid Help?

Due to distance, increasing care recipient needs, or other obligations, you may need or want to hire help. Depending on the care recipient's condition, you may consider paying a personal friend, family member, homemaker, or licensed nurse for their assistance. As the principal caregiver, you remain in charge. This book deals with crafting critical conversations and detailed understanding of this type conversation is very crucial to a successful outcome. This is different than hiring someone to help with a project. It's highly personal for both of you and the care recipient.

Here are two different models of homecare services delivery you can investigate. The first is where the home care provider has an employer/employee model, and the second is a domestic referral agencies or independent contracting, often called the domestic registry model.

- With the employer model, you engage with a provider that is generally bonded and insured, offers comprehensive orientation with in-depth caregiver training, takes care of any legal issues that occur should the caregiver or client be injured in the job, and provides ongoing supervision.

- The Registered and Independent Contracting models are generally agencies or organizations that help families locate a caregiver and place one in a client's home on an independent-contractor basis. Registries do not serve as an employer, nor can they take responsibility for supervision. That means you are liable for payroll taxes and possible work-related injuries of the caregiver as part of this model, so basically, the family is directly responsible as the employer of the caregiver.

Here are some additional considerations:

- You will need to discuss, or at the least explain to the care recipient, what the paid hired caregiver will and will not do.
- Develop a list of responsibilities/duties in advance, since all parties need to understand the expectation of service. This will also allow the provider, prospective agency, or independent contractor to select a good fit.
- Work together on a list of things that won't work for the care recipient. There may be taboo topics or memorabilia that must not be touched. Cover physical attributes. For example, does one of them smoke, does the helper wear a uniform, are they strong enough to lift your loved one? Cover social aspects. Will the helper cook things that your loved one will eat, do they drive, and will they refuse gifts from the care recipient, etc.?
- If you hire an independent contractor, experience counts. Check referrals and set a pre-determined check-in schedule, so it is clear you are in charge.
- Periodically, check-in with your loved one as well.
- In either care, both parties should expect to sign a contract. Appendix C provides a link to check if the caregiver is

considered an employee or independent contractor and an insightful article on the topic as well.

Someone Feels That They Live Too Far Away to Participate

- The role of a long distance caregiver should be practical and allow for participation. If you are or expect to be a long distance, sole, or alpha child for a loved one, contact police or first responders and ask what they advise. You should provide them or any organization they suggest with the name, address, or contact information for the older person as well as yourself.

- Consider investigating if there is a community or faith-based organization that will provide temporary assistance, giving you time to travel to help your loved one.

- Many financial and decision-making roles do not depend upon being close-by. Schedule inclusive zoom calls, webinars, or facetime calls to see how things are going.

- There are apps that track financial behavior and alert you if elder abuse is suspected or if changes in financial patterns are out of the norm. This may be especially important for high net worth families. (See Appendix C.)

All the Funding Options Feel Unaffordable

I feel like the options to fund extended care don't fit in our budget, so we'll leave it for later.

- The better question is "can you afford to wait?" It is common to confuse the cost of offsetting the risk with the actual cost-of-care. It is helpful to look at the rate at which the cost-of-care has increased over specific time periods. This moves the discussion from guessing to factual information.

- The cost-of-care can vary significantly depending on several factors, including the type of care needed, duration of care, type of facility, and the individual's health condition. Costs also vary widely depending on your location. While services tend to be more expensive in urban areas and less expensive in rural regions, accessibility can be a factor. (See Appendix C for cost-of-care sites).

Where's the Money Coming From?

The Cost-of-Care depends on many variables.

- First, gather some realistic estimates. Use one of the websites that offers current costs as well as estimated future costs. Several links can be found in Appendix C.

Once a realistic estimate is determined, a parent may not want to reveal their resources. To avoid prying, explore locations where they or you expect to be in ten, twenty, or thirty years.

- If where the parent will live has not been determined, use a calculator to determine the cost of potential living arrangements. Consider what is involved in different scenarios, such as:
    - Staying in their current home (consider upgrades or modification costs and disruptions)
    - Moving closer to family or into a family member's home (include sale or relocation costs and impact on family's current lifestyle)
    - Moving to a home with a more accommodating layout and/or less upkeep (consider costs to sell current home or terminate a lease and relocation costs. Consider down payment or ongoing charges for the new residence).
    - Moving to a housing community that offers care services, amenities, and home maintenance (costs to sell current home,

selection of amenities, can the housing selection handle longer term or increasing care needs or will an additional solution be needed?)

o Moving to a facility that accommodates gradually increasing care needs (investigate down payments and ongoing costs, which may be subject to increases and charges for additional services).

My Parent is Uninsurable

There is no point in doing the three steps for my uninsurable parent.

The three steps are not about insurance. They're about planning.

- As part of the planning exercise, you will learn about options that may suit uninsurable individuals, those who don't want or need additional insurance, or those with budget constraints.

- The three steps focus on different aspects of planning for different ages and stages, considering health, budget, personal and professional support, services, and responsibilities.

I Am Confused about the Types of Insurance

If you don't do insurance for a living, find an agent who does!

- The Care Guide serves as a fact finder for an agent or financial professional. It helps him/her to uncover appropriate options. Remind him/her to eliminate insurance and healthcare jargon and terminology. You want to understand what the insurance option does and does not do.

- The importance of care coordination cannot be overemphasized. Care coordination offers a holistic approach to the caregiving journey, as opposed to care management that focuses on high-touch, episodic encounters. Care coordination is a benefit usually included in Traditional LTC and some Hybrid or Combination insurance policies. For those who don't include this benefit, the CPT can access public facsimiles, like an area agency on aging to help navigate the caregiving journey. An area agency on aging (AAA) is a public or private non-profit agency, designated by the state to address the needs and concerns of all older persons at the regional and local levels.

- Ask lots of questions! Ask specific questions about benefit triggers that release the benefit for use, ask about tax codes and guarantees. There is no such thing as an unimportant question.

Chapter 10

Concluding Thoughts and Encouragement

You are faced with a dramatically different choice: plan or panic. I hope you have gained some knowledge, direction, and practical ideas to kick off critical extended care planning conversations. Start your caregiver journey with a plan instead of concern, confusion, and chaos!

Many of us will join the ranks of the shadow caregiving system and the associated shadow caregiving economy, which is OK if your plan limits your exposure to what you can and want to do and not what you must do.

Step into a plan by assembling a Care Guide to document important facts and thoughts, avoid chaos by building a Care Squad enabling others to be supportive, and forming a Care Planning Team to uncover the right options to offset what promises to be a very trying and expensive experience without a plan.

I understand this is not easy topic for either caregiver or potential care recipient, so select, personalize, or modify the suggestions to overcome objections and challenges to conversations, identify and share some of the stories, access the resources in the appendixes to continue to explore, learn and move towards building your family's best possible physical, psychological, and financial extended care plan.

The responses to challenges and objections I have offered are only from my limited perspective. If I have missed something or you need my support, please reach out to me at carroll@thecaringconversation.com I encourage you to adopt an attitude that recognizes that successful planning is a process.

To get the most out of this book, ask yourself, "What have I learned that will work for my situation?" My ultimate goal is to give you the tools and ideas to craft critical conversations to create a life enhancing extended care plan, put your mind at ease, and live a life of courage, hope, joy, and caring.

Section III

APPENDIX A: Care Guide Content List

Selecting from this basic list to create your personal Care Guide is easier if you break it down into categories and fill it in overtime. You may find you want to include things that are not listed below. I suggest that you start with things that are needed or most helpful in an emergency healthcare situation.

Be sure to keep your Care Guide in a safe, fireproof place, or with strong digital security in an electronic version. Consider carefully with whom you want to share the Care Guide or grant digital access to its contents. In the context of this list, "your" applies to the owner of the Care Guide. Outside of a pending emergency, creating a Care Guide is a gradual process, but remember to periodically update it.

Care Guide App

- www.getprismm.com A Prismm account is a digital Care Guide vault for your most important documents and financial information. Why do you store documents in a safe but accessible place? Because you and/or your caregiver need them for your physical and financial wellbeing.

Basic Legal Documents

- This book is an outstanding, easy to read excellent resource. Cathy Sikorski, Esq. *12 Conversations: How to Talk to Almost Anyone About Long-Term Care*, Corner Office Books, 2021
- A will is a legal document which designates your executor(s) and directs how your assets should be distributed after you have passed on.
- A living will is a written statement that expresses your wishes in regard to your medical treatment in the event that you are unable to express informed consent.
- A medical power of attorney which may also be called a durable healthcare power of attorney or a healthcare proxy grants someone the power to make medical decisions for you if you become incapacitated.
- A durable general power of attorney authorizes your designee to manage your assets if you are not able to do so.

Personal Contact Information

- Your legal name, date of birth, and legal (and current if different) residence
- Your place of birth, your parent's names, and family ancestry
- Spouse, partner, significant other's legal name, date of birth, and legal and current residence
- Phone numbers and access codes for you and those who you want to be contacted should be listed. Note all the numbers and access codes you use at home, at work, while on vacation, and visiting with friends or if a family member needs to access your home in your absence. For example, list landlines, cell phones, computers, tablets, alarm codes, pagers, internet access carriers, etc.
- If you have a personal safe or safe deposit box at a bank that contains your important documents, list the location, combination or access code. In the case of a bank or other type of vault, make sure the institution knows that you authorize this person to gain access and that they know where the key to open your box or container is kept.
- Health history. Include prior hospital stays, medications, chronic conditions, implanted devices, joint replacements, dental visits, vision and hearing information, immune deficiencies, or illness complications.

- Pet(s). Indicate who will take care of the pet in your absence, and if compensation is involved, how it will be handled.
- Indicate your primary and secondary language (if applicable).

Professional Contact Information

- This list should include contact information for doctors, specialists, pharmacy or mail-in pharmacy, and hospital preference.
- You should list your medical conditions, allergies, and the frequency and location of any special treatments you regularly undergo (such as dialysis).
- List your advisors, including a CPA or tax consultant, attorney or legal counsel, retirement or investment advisor, and financial and insurance agent(s).

Financial Worksheet

- Assets – list or include copies of statements indicating type, issuing institution, and contact information for investments, savings accounts, insurances (type and contact information), stocks, securities, bank or custodial accounts, retirement assets, military, government, or employment pension or benefits, savings and investments, rewards program, property ownership, foreign assets, or trusts. Where appropriate, you may want to indicate beneficiaries for the various assets.

- Debts – list liabilities for yourself and anyone for whom you are responsible. Include statements indicating type, institution, and contact information for debts including credit and debit card, mortgages, leases, foreign debt, subscriptions, lawsuits, personal or business insurance payments, health care payments, home equity, lines of credit, student loans, liens, borrowed items, storage facility, unit number or location and cost, safety deposit unit location and cost, pet care insurance or bills, loans, payment plans, membership dues, joint or individual credit card balances, software, phone, computer and streaming device charges.

- Other obligations or payments made for other family members (such as leases, lawsuit settlements, etc.)

Personal Documents

- Educational savings plans for which you are the custodian or payor (for example: a Trust or 529 plan)
- Organ donation forms
- Business or family partnerships or LLC
- Deeds to real property and property tax payments

- Vehicle titles (cars, boat, airplane, street legal golf carts, recreation vehicles, etc.)
- Marriage license, divorce or separation agreement, child support agreement, post or pre-nuptial agreement
- Birth certificate, adoption papers, guardianship document, citizen or visa documents, passports
- Burial, cremation, or pre-need documents
- Insurances (personal, home, valuables)
- Military service (branch, dates of separation from service, or date of retirement)
- Tax returns
- Veterinarian contact
- Details of parental or child responsibilities

Business Documents

- Current W-2 employer or consultant agreement
- Business owner or partnership
- Buy-sell (list funding mechanism and triggers) or overhead expense agreement
- Disability insurance
- Tax returns
- Lawsuits or legal disputes

APPENDIX B: Private and Public Funding Sources and Planning Options

For those in good or relatively good health:

- Insurance options:
    - Traditional long-term care (TLTC)
    - Workplace/group long-term care (GLTC)
    - Life insurance with LTC riders or LTC with life insurance
    - Annuities with LTC riders
    - Term Insurance with LTC endorsement
    - Whole life and universal life insurance

For those with some health issues or budget concerns:

- Insurance and non-insurance options include:
    - Single Premium Immediate Annuity (SPIA) or Medicaid Qualified Annuity
    - Veteran's benefits
    - Medicare (benefits are extremely limited)

- Reverse mortgage (home equity conversion mortgage)
- Life settlement
- Short-term care

For those who meet the definition of impoverished:

- Long-term services and supports
- Medicaid
- City, county, and state programs

For many, but not all:

- Publicly funded state program

APPENDIX C: Resource Links

Cost-of-Care sites:

- https://www.genworth.com/aging-and-you/finances/cost-of-care.html
- https://www.whatcarecosts.com/lincoln
- https://caregiveradvocate.com/johnhancock-cost-of-care/wellness/cost-care-public
- https://www.mutualofomaha.com/long-term-care-insurance/calculator
- https://www.alz.org/help-support/caregiving/financial-legal-planning/planning-for-care-costs

Social Security sites:

- https://www.ssa.gov/oact/anypia/index.html
- https://www.ssa.gov/oact/quickcalc/early_late.html#calculator

Provides rough estimates of your retirement benefit based on your current earnings when you apply at different times between sixty-two and seventy.

- https://search.ssa.gov/search?affiliate=ssa&sort_by=&query=longevity+calcullator&commit=Search

   Longevity calculator

- https://www.ssa.gov/medicare/plan/when-to-sign-up

   It is important to sign up promptly and correctly.

- https://www.ssa.gov/prepare/government-and-foreign-pensions

   See how pensions may affect social security benefits.

Caregiver Advice, Support, and Resources

- https://www.thecaringconversation.com (books and information on caregiving)
- https://getprismm.com (Care Guide planning platform)
- https://carerightinc.com (Crisis planning expert)
- https://www.myfloc.com (elder financial abuse or fraud prevention platform)
- https://www.caregiving.com/posts/how-to-help-a-family-caregiver
- https://searchfindhelp.org
- https://www.caregiver.org/connecting-caregivers/services-by-state

- https://retirement-insight.com/the-value-of-safe-home-care/
- https://www.sroke.org/en/help-and-support/for-family-caregivers
- https://aarp.org AARP is the nation's largest nonprofit, nonpartisan organization dedicated to empowering Americans over fifty years to choose how they live as they age.
- https://www.getcarefull.com This app tracks financial behavior that signals if elder abuse is suspected or if changes in financial patterns are out of the norm.
- https://asaging.org
- https://www.councilonaging.org
- https://order.nia.nih.gov/ The National Institute on Aging (NIA) leads a broad scientific effort to understand the nature of aging and to extend the healthy, active years of life. The NIA is the primary federal agency supporting and conducting Alzheimer's disease research.
- https://acl.gov (Health and Human Services Department)

An area agency on aging (AAA) is a public or private non-profit agency, designated by the state to address the needs and concerns of all older persons at the regional and local levels. Area agency on aging is a generic term—specific names of local AAAs may vary. AAAs are primarily responsible for a geographic area, also known as a PSA, that is either a city, a single county, or a multi-county district. AAAs coordinate and offer services that help older adults remain in their homes, if that is their preference.

- https://www.consumerfinance.gov/consumer-tools/managing-someone-elses-money/ Includes easy-to-understand guides to help financial caregivers.

Additional Resources

- https://www.medicare.gov/what-medicare-covers/whats-not-covered-by-part-a-part-b
- https://www.ssa.gov/medicare/plan/when-to-sign-up
- https://www.medicare.gov/coverage/yearly-wellness-visits
- https://www.medicare.gov/coverage/durable-medical-dme-coverage
- http://www.medicare.gov/coverage/home-health-services
- https://www.alz.org (Alzheimer's Association)
- https://www.alzinc.org (Alzheimer's Association)

- https://www.themost-affordable-places-in-the-US-to-retire (location)
- https://eldercare.acl.gov/Public/Index.aspx (Eldercare locator sponsored by the U.S. Administration on Aging)
- https://www.caregiver.org/resource/personal-care-agreements/
- https://www.medicaidplanningassistance.org/personal-care-agreements/
- https://eforms.com/ (caregiver agreement template)
- www.opioidfinancialawareness.com (pharmaceutical addiction)
- https://www.ssa.gov/prepare/plan-retirement
- https://www.ssa.gov/manage-benefits/request-withhold-taxes
- https://www.ssa.gov/prepare/government-and-foreign-pensions
- https://www.ssa.gov/prepare/special-earnings (While Social Security earnings are calculated the same way for most American workers, there are some types of earnings that have additional rules.)

About the Author

Carroll S. Golden is a speaker and consultant devoted to helping professionals, individuals, and families plan for a smooth and loving transition when extended care needs arise.

Carroll often says that when she asks a caregiver what they do, they likely respond with a current or past job rather than "I'm my parent's caregiver." Carroll hears many stories about caregiver hardships. Although a degree of emotional and financial stress is unavoidable, those caregiving experiences either brought families closer together or tore them apart. Her own personal experience taught her that the differential is whether there are critical conversations to put an extended care plan in place or if those critical planning conversations are off-limits. Her extensive expertise inspired her to author her inaugural book, *How Not To Tear Your Family Apart*, a valuable resource for professionals seeking a comprehensive understanding of multigenerational limited, extended, and long-term care planning.

As the Executive Director of the National Association of Insurance and Financial Advisors Specialty Centers, Carroll oversees the Limited and Extended Care Planning Center and the Legislative Working Group which discusses various legislation, studies, proposals, and initiatives related to state publicly funded long-term care programs.

A well-respected industry thought leader, executive positions with insurers and distributors, involvement in public policy and consumer advocacy, interviews, presentations, podcasts, and industry conference leadership roles give Carroll a holistic view of limited, extended, and long-term care planning.

Carroll has earned several designations throughout her career:
- Chartered Life Underwriter® (CLU®) (American College of Financial Services)
- Chartered Financial Consultant® (ChFC®) (American College of Financial Services)
- Certified in Long-Term Care® (CLTC®) (Corporation for Certification for Long-Term Care)
- Long-Term Care Professional® (LTCP®) (America's Health Insurance Plans (AHIP)
- Chartered Advisor in Senior Living® (CASL®) (American College of Financial Services)
- Chartered Mutual Fund Counselor (CMFC) (College for Financial Planning)
- Fellow, Life Management Institute® (FLMI®) (Life Office Management Association (LOMA)
- *Associate, Customer Service*™ (ACS®) (Life Office Management Association (LOMA)
- Life and Annuity Certified Professional® (LACP®) (National Association of Insurance and Financial Advisors (NAIFA)

Carroll actively participates in the long-term care industry and has served in key leadership roles.
- Former Chapter President Society of Financial Service Professionals (FSP)
- Chairperson for the Society of Actuaries® (SOA) Fifth Long-term Care Conference

- Chairperson for the Intercompany Long-Term Care Insurance Conference (ILTCI)
- Member of the Executive Board of ILTCI
- Author and presenter of the Long-Term Care Insurance module for the Online Elder Planning Specialist course offered to members of the Financial Planning Association® (FPA®).
- Teaches State Continuing Education (CE) classes
- Speaker for Betty Meredith's Retirement Speakers Bureau
- Presenter at the 2022 Annual Financial Planning Association® Conference

In conjunction with the extended care story in her second book, an Amazon bestseller, *How Not to Pull Your Family Apart: A Practical Guide to Caregiving and Financial Stability*, Carroll writes a weekly blog linking current newsworthy extended care issues and planning options to the book's story. They are available, along with all of her books, at www.thecaringconversation.com or wherever you purchase your books.